SEGURA • ROSENBERG • EISMA • HERMS • MORELLI

THE ARCHIES

VOLUME TWO

D1340532

SOUTHWARK LIBRARIES

SK 2687264 1

THE ARCHIES

VOLUME TWO

STORY BY
ALEX SEGURA AND
MATTHEW ROSENBERG

ART BY
JOE EISMA

LETTERING BY
JACK MORELLI

COLORS BY
MATT HERMS

EDITOR-IN-CHIEF
VICTOR GORELICK

EDITORS:
VINCENT LOVALLO AND
JAMIE LEE ROTANTE

PUBLISHER
JON GOLDWATER

ASSOCIATE EDITOR:
STEPHEN OSWALD

GRAPHIC DESIGN:
KARI MCLACHLAN

A TALE OF BLOWN AMPS AND BUSTED FRIENDSHIPS

When we set out to tell the story of the Archies, the creative team—with the support of Archie Publisher/CEO Jon Goldwater and the entire team at Archie Comics—had two big goals: to get as many cool, wow-type guest stars as possible and, on a more challenging level, to make the entire season tell one, long, meaningful story.

Neither job was easy, but one was more subtle. On the surface, the comic—co-written by me and my friend Matt Rosenberg, with killer art by Joe Eisma, Matt Herms and Jack Morelli—was about pairing the Archies (Archie, Betty and Veronica, Jughead, and Reggie) with big-name acts. In that regard, we'd hit paydirt from the beginning—locking in groups like CHVRCHES, the Monkees, Blondie, Speedy Ortiz and Tegan and Sara. Everyone was excited to be a part of the comic, and they were all engaged partners—giving suggestions, ideas, promoting the heck out of the books and enjoying the ride. At the end of the day, the books were meant to be fun—and the bands got that.

The collection you hold in your hand contains the final few issues of the series, including a dream issue where the kids find themselves face-to-face with the pre-Fab Four, a story where Tegan and Sara experience an Archies member quitting and one tale where the legendary Blondie produce the Archies record. Again, fun. But underneath the surface of music video hype was a more personal story, about five friends setting out on a big adventure and coming to terms with the fact that maybe, just maybe, it wasn't all going to turn out exactly as they'd hoped.

Being in a band is tough. Friendships and romance are not easy, either. Especially when you're teenager, still figuring out who you are. So, while the Archies was always about the big-screen adventures —about the unbelievable crossovers and cameos—it was also a book about growing up and dealing with the inevitable setbacks of life. I like to think we did our best to reflect both things, and I hope you enjoy the ride.

Alex Segura
Co-Writer, THE ARCHIES

Special Thanks:

CHVRCHES and Campbell McNeil, Melissa Schienberg, Dana Erickson, Danny Rogers

Tegan and Sara and Bobbie Gale, Piers Henwood

The Monkees, Rhino Records and John Hughes, Jason Elzy

Blondie and Thomas Manzi

Speedy Ortiz and Sadie Dupuis

THAT WAS... WEIRD.

ARCHIEKINS, YOU ARE A MESS!

WHAT...?

WE'RE IN THE MIDDLE OF A SONG!

YES. JUST STRUM THAT STUPID GUITAR OF YOURS.

WAIT-- *LOOK!* THEY'VE GOT HIM!

GOT WHO?!

The Archies

IS THAT... *DAVY JONES?!*

GET UP, STAND UP, KID.

I *AM* STANDING UP!

EXIT

HE'S GONE!

HEY...HEY... AREN'T YOU *THE MONKEES?*

NO *WAY!* THEY HAD *CHEESEDOGS* HERE?!

YES, WE ARE.

WHAT WAS HAPPENING WITH THAT VAN?

THEY SEEMED TO BE IN A HURRY.

WE WERE PLAYING A GIG AND TWO CREEPS GRABBED SOME GUY.

SOME CUTE, SMALL BOY WITH A CHARMING SMILE.

Oh, THAT MUST HAVE BEEN DAVY!

PEOPLE TRY TO KIDNAP HIM ALL THE TIME!

MAKE YOURSELVES COMFORTABLE!

WE'LL BE RIGHT BACK.

THIS PLACE IS AMAZING.

WE ARE READY!

THE READIEST!

SUPER-READY!

WHAT'S WITH THE COSTUMES?

WHY DOES ALL THE FOOD TASTE ...OLD?

DIDN'T YOU GET YOUR COSTUMES?

COSTUMES?

YEAH! FOR OUR DETECTIVE MISSION!

WHERE DID THIS EVEN COME FROM?

A THRIFT STORE, IT SMELLS LIKE.

I'D BLAME ALL THIS ON FOOD POISONING, BUT IT WAS WEIRD *BEFORE* I ATE THAT SAND-WICH.

SAVE THE TEXAS PRAIRIE CHICKEN!

WOW, SECURITY LOOKS TOUGH.

Umm... I DIDN'T THINK "THE VOLCANO" WAS A *REAL* VOLCANO.

SOLD OUT!

I'M NOT SURE HOW WE CAN GET IN.

I HAVE AN IDEA!

TA-*DA!*

HEY, HOW DID YOU GUYS DO THAT?!

COME ON, ARCHIE. DON'T BE DULL. YOU KNOW SABRINA TAUGHT ME SOME MAGIC.

SABRINA TAUGHT YOU *WHAT?!*

WHO'S *SABRINA?*

EVERYONE IN!

HEY, THIS IS GREAT!

NO. IT ISN'T.

HIS VOICE... IT'S SO FAMILIAR.

...SUGAR, SUGAR...

IT'S DAVY!

HEY! HE'S BACK HERE... OOH.

THAT'S PRETTY WEIRD, RIGHT?

NOT REALLY.

WE HAVE TO SAVE HIM!

THOSE GORILLAS HAVE HIM TIED UP PRETTY GOOD AND THEY'RE NOT GOING TO LET HIM GO. EVEN WITH DAVY FAKING IT FOR THEM, THE CROWD LOVES IT.

WELL, WE'LL JUST HAVE TO SHOW THE CROWD WHAT A REAL BAND SOUNDS LIKE.

BUT HOW?

BATTLE OF THE BANDS!

DID YOU JUST *MAGIC* OUR INSTRUMENTS ONTO US?

I GUESS I DID.

OKAY.

HEY!

THAT'S ENOUGH! YOU STUPID KIDS ARE GOING TO RUIN EVERYTHING!

BOO! BOOOOO!

BIG TIME RECORDS SPENT A LOT OF MONEY FIGURING OUT HOW TO SELL RECORDS TO ALL THESE IDIOTS. IT TURNS OUT KIDS TODAY ARE TOO STUPID TO REALIZE THAT THEY ARE LISTENING TO MANUFACTURED JUNK!

OH, WILL YOU MORONS SHUT UP FOR--

BONK

THIS NEXT SONNNNNGGG IS... >WHIRR< THIS NEXT SONNNNGGGG IS... >WHIRR<

...IS WHAT?

TONY WAS A ROBOT?!

FIGURES.

I'VE JUST PICKED UP A FAULT IN THE AE-35 UNIT. IT'S GOING TO GO 100% FAILURE WITHIN 72 HOURS.

NOW LET'S GO FREE THE CUTE BOY!

DAVY. STAND UP!

I AM STANDING.

YOU'RE FREE?!

Oh, YEAH. I WAS ONLY STICKING AROUND BECAUSE THEY TOLD ME THEY'D BUY ME DINNER AFTER THIS.

WE'RE SO HAPPY YOU'RE OKAY!

ACK!

OOOh! HE'S POCKET-SIZED!

WHAT A CRAZY DAY. GORILLAS, ROBOTS, KIDNAPPINGS, VOLCANOES.

WHO'S HE TALKING TO?

I DON'T SEE ANYONE OUT THERE.

IF HE THINKS TODAY WAS CRAZY, HE SHOULD'VE SEEN WHAT WE DID YESTER-DAY.

HE KNOWS THIS IS ALL A DREAM, RIGHT?

NOT THAT I DON'T APPRECIATE THE DARING RESCUE AND ALL, BUT WEREN'T YOU IN THE MIDDLE OF A SHOW WHEN THIS ALL STARTED?

OUR SHOW!!

I KNOW IT'S GOOD TO LEAVE THE AUDIENCE WANTING MORE...

ACTUALLY, WE LIKE TO LEAVE THEM WANTING LESS.

ISSUE FIVE

GUYS, RELAX. WE'LL GET BETTER.

WILL WE? WE'RE CERTAINLY NOWHERE NEAR READY FOR THE SHOW I BOOKED IN L.A.

WE'RE NOT READY TO PLAY SHOWS IN RIVERDALE!

JUG, WHAT DO YOU THINK? YOU'RE BEING AWFUL QUIET.

JUG?

I CAN'T BE GOING CRAZY, RIGHT? WE WILL GET BETTER. WE HAVE TO.

WELL...

WHAT? COME ON, BETTS. GIVE IT TO ME STRAIGHT.

I'M...I'M STARTING TO THINK THEY'RE RIGHT, ARCHIE.

KANSAS CITY.

WE WEREN'T THE ONLY CONCERNED PARTIES, EITHER.

LISTEN, ARCHIE, WE HAVE TO TALK.

SURE, OKAY.

I HAVE SOME GOOD NEWS.

OH, GREAT. WOW. WE COULD REALLY USE IT.

OKAY, WELL, I ALSO HAVE SOME BAD NEWS. GOOD NEWS--I GOT THE BINGOES ONTO A CANADIAN TOUR, WHICH WILL FUND OUR TRIP TO THE WEST COAST AND LET US HOP DOWN TO CALIFORNIA IN A FEW WEEKS.

THAT'S PERFECT! THAT'LL GET US RIGHT TO WHERE WE NEED TO BE!

WELL, YEAH. BUT I'M NOT SURE THAT TOUR INCLUDES YOU GUYS.

WHAT... WHAT DO YOU MEAN?

THE ARCHIES ARE... JUST NOT ANY GOOD, MAN. I'M SORRY.

UNLESS SOMETHING CHANGES, YOU WON'T BE COMING TO CANADA WITH US.

BINGO HAD SOME DOUBTS ABOUT US OPENING FOR NOT ONLY *THE BINGOES*, BUT A MAJOR GROUP LIKE *TEGAN AND SARA*.

I--I LOVE YOU GUYS. THAT'S ALL I CAN SAY.

DON'T RUIN THIS FOR ME.

HEY GUYS, HI.

EXCITED TO BE ON THE BILL WITH YOU.

HOW DID *WE* GET ON THIS BILL?

PITY, I GUESS.

REGGIE'S HALF RIGHT. BINGO DID FEEL BAD FOR TRYING TO GET US OFF THE TOUR.

BUT NOT BAD ENOUGH TO SKIP TRYING TO GET US *OFF* THE BILL.

HEY, *JOSIE!* HOW'S IT--

WHAT? OH, YEAH, NO WORRIES. I GET IT.

JINX! HEY, IT WAS SO GREAT TO--

NO, NO, I HEAR YOU. YOU'RE BUSY. AH, OKAY.

OKAY, YOU GUYS ARE *ON*. BUT THIS IS YOUR LAST SHOT.

COULDN'T FIND ANYONE ELSE, EH?

BEST I COULD DO WAS TEDDY TAMBOURINE READING BEAT POETRY.

SOMEWHERE NEAR BOISE.

I THOUGHT OPENING FOR TEGAN AND SARA WOULD BE WHAT WE NEEDED TO JUMP-START THE BAND.

NO *WAY* ARE WE READY FOR THIS.

I THINK RON IS RIGHT, ARCHIE. WE SHOULD HAVE TALKED ABOUT IT BEFORE YOU SAID YES.

WHO DEPUTIZED YOU TO BE OVERLORD OF THE BAND? ALSO, CANADA?

I WAS WRONG.

I'M SICK OF THIS.

WHAT DO YOU MEAN?

EVERYTHING. WE'RE JUST PUTTERING ALONG, GRIPING AND SNIPING AT EACH OTHER. IT'S NOT EVEN FUN TO EAT ON THE ROAD ANYMORE.

FOR ONCE, I AGREE WITH LUNKHEAD. THE NOVELTY WORE OFF PRETTY FAST ON THIS WHOLE "TOURING" THING.

SO, WE PLAYED THE SHOW.

THIS SONG IS, UH...

NEXT TO NOTHING...!

UM, 'NEXT TO NOTHING,' YEAH!

WELL, PLAYED IS RELATIVE.

STANDING NEXT TO NOTHING ALL OVER AGAIN...!

ACK, WHOOPS!

STARTED OUT WITH SOMETHING -- NOW THERE'S NOTHIN' AGAIIIIIN!

OH, WHATEVER.

WHAT A LOT OF PEOPLE DON'T GET IS THAT JUGHEAD'S A GREAT, GREAT DRUMMER.

THAT'S IT...!

AND, IF YOU KNOW ANYTHING ABOUT BEING IN A BAND, YOU KNOW A RELIABLE, TALENTED AND EASYGOING DRUMMER IS LIKE A UNICORN--RARE, MAGICAL AND HARD TO HOLD ONTO.

I CAN'T DEAL WITH THIS ANY-MORE...

I QUIT!!

AND WE JUST LOST OURS.

SO, IT WAS SCRAMBLE TIME.

WHAT DO WE DO NOW? JUGHEAD'S AWOL.

I MEAN, I CAN KEEP A BEAT.

I THINK.

WHAT ABOUT A DRUM MACHINE?

LIKE A ROBOT?

NO, LIKE, ELECTRONIC DRUMS. I THINK I HAVE ROOM ON MY CARD.

HEARD *THAT* STORY BEFORE.

ELSEWHERE IN VANCOUVER.

corduroy

AND NOW, OUR NEXT PERFORMER, FROM THE STATES...

I MEAN, I HATE TO SAY IT, *BUT*...

THEY WERE KIND OF TERRIBLE.

THEY'VE JUST HAD A BAD RUN, IS ALL. I THINK THEY CAN FIX IT.

LOOK, BINGO, IT'S YOUR CALL. WE GAVE YOU TWO SLOTS.

AND WE *TOTALLY* GET WANTING TO SUPPORT YOUR FRIENDS.

I MEAN, WE LIKE THE ARCHIES. WE LIKED WHAT WE'D HEARD.

BUT...?

NOTHING. WE JUST NEED TO FIGURE IT OUT.

THEIR SET LAST NIGHT WAS... *ROUGH.*

TAP TAP TIPPY-TAP-TAP

HEY, GUYS, HOLD UP--ARE YOU HEARING THAT?

...GOING BY THE NAME FPJ, HE'S GOING TO PERFORM SOME DRUM MUSIC FOR YOU. DON'T FORGET TO TIP YOUR SERVERS, FOLKS.

BRADDA-BRADDA-BUM-BUM-*BAP*

DRUM SOLO? PRETTY BRAVE.

HE'S GOT *MY* ATTENTION.

IS THAT...?

Tik Tik Tik

I'M GONNA PLAY A FEW QUICK SONGS I WROTE. HOPE YOU DIG 'EM.

TAKKA-TAKKA-TAK-*DRRRAP*

TSS-TSS-TAP-TAP-*TRAPPA-TAP*

WE HAVE TO MEET THIS GUY.

WHOA! HOW RANDOM IS THIS?

TIP-TIP-TAPPY-TAP-TSSS-TSS-*BOOM*

WAIT... WE *HAVE* MET THIS GUY.

JUGHEAD?!

THAT WAS...

...AMAZING. YOU'RE *GREAT!*

THANKS.

ARE YOU STILL WITH THE ARCHIES?

NAH.

WANNA PLAY SOME MUSIC WITH US LATER?

SURE, OKAY.

HEY.

YOU FIND JUGHEAD?

YEAH, BUT HE'S NOT COMING BACK.

WE ALL KINDA FIGURED THAT. I AM GOING TO REGRET SAYING IT, BUT I'M GOING TO MISS THAT GOOF.

YEAH, WELL...IF THE VAN IS ALL LOADED UP I THINK WE SHOULD HIT THE ROAD. IT'S A FEW DAYS DRIVE BACK TO RIVERDALE.

YEAH, SO, WE TALKED ABOUT IT. WE WANT TO KEEP GOING.

YOU WHAT?

THE BAND ISN'T CALLED 'THE JUGHEADS'... EVEN THOUGH THAT IS A BETTER NAME. WE'RE NOT QUITTERS. SO WHY SHOULD WE QUIT?

HEY ARCHIES! SO I GUESS THIS IS GOODBYE. IT WAS REAL--

WE'RE FINISHING THE TOUR...I MEAN... UNLESS WE'RE KICKED OFF?

WELL NO, BUT...YOU GUYS WERE PRETTY ROUGH BEFORE. HOW'S THIS GOING TO WORK NOW?

LET'S FIND OUT!

ONE, TWO, THREE, FOUR!

C'MON! GET INTO IT!

YOU WORRY ABOUT HITTING THE *RIGHT NOTES*, ANDREWS!

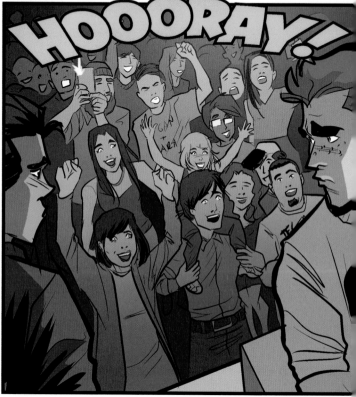

HOOORAY!

TO BE CONTINUED...

ISSUE SIX

WE HAD A GREAT SHOW WITH TEGAN AND SARA A FEW WEEKS AGO--I THOUGHT IT'D FIX ALL OUR PROBLEMS.

INSTEAD, I KIND OF CREATED MORE.

JUGHEAD'S STILL GONE. I KNOW HE'S IN L.A. SOMEWHERE, BUT IT'S CLEAR HE DOESN'T WANT TO BE ONE OF *THE ARCHIES* ANY-MORE.

AND, I, UH, KIND OF HOOKED UP WITH VERONICA AFTER A SHOW IN SAN DIEGO.

SO--BETTY'S NOT REALLY TALKING TO ME, NEITHER IS VERONICA AND JUGHEAD'S DITCHED US. I GUESS THINGS *COULD* BE WORSE?

THE NEXT NIGHT, WE WRAPPED UP A NOT-TERRIBLE SHOW AT *LOS GLOBOS*. BUT THAT WAS JUST THE OPENING ACT.

BETTY, WE NEED TO TALK.

NO, WE DON'T. SERIOUSLY. IT'S FINE. I DON'T CARE.

I *DO* CARE, THOUGH. AND I DON'T WANT TO FALL BACK INTO OLD RIVERDALE BEHAVIORS.

WHAT DO YOU MEAN?

BETTY, IT HAPPENED. YOU SAW IT. I COULD CALL IT A MOMENT OF WEAKNESS OR LAPSE OR WHATEVER, BUT THAT WOULDN'T BE FAIR TO YOU OR EVEN ARCHIE.

I DON'T CARE, OKAY? YOU MAKE A NICE PAIR. GO FORTH AND BE COUPLE-Y.

NOT THE POINT. WHATEVER HAPPENS BETWEEN ARCHIE AND ME, OR ARCHIE AND YOU--YOU'RE MY BEST FRIEND. THAT'S MY PRIORITY. THAT'S WHAT I WANTED TO SAY.

O-OKAY.

WE'RE ALL WIPED-- SHORT ON SLEEP, EXHAUSTED FROM PLAYING AND DOWN A MEMBER.

BUT WE'RE GONNA MAKE A RECORD.

THAT'S PRETTY COOL.

GUYS. THIS IS IT. I KNOW WE'RE DOWN A DRUMMER. I KNOW YOU DON'T REALLY SEEM TO LIKE ME MUCH.

BUT THIS IS WHAT WE'VE BEEN WORKING FOR SINCE WE GOT TOGETHER THAT NIGHT AT THE JACKPOT.

WE CAN DO THIS. RIGHT?

SURE, OKAY.

LODGES CAN DO ANY- THING.

IS IT JUST ME OR IS THIS PLACE KIND OF A DUMP?

HERE GOES NOTHING.

WAITRESS? I NEVER GOT MY CURLY FRIES!

SORRY ABOUT THAT. I WASN'T SURE...YOU'D REALLY NEED THEM.

I DO.

COMING RIGHT UP.

THANKS. I LIKE TO PUT THEM ON MY BURGERS, SO--

YOU'RE REALLY *GROSS*, YOU KNOW THAT?

HOW'D YOU FIND ME?

I'M RICH. I CAN DO ANYTHING.

YOU'VE BEEN TO EVERY BURGER SPOT IN THE VALLEY, HAVEN'T YOU?

YUP.

LUCKY.

COME BACK TO THE BAND.

WHY WOULD I DO THAT?

BECAUSE YOU WANT TO PLAY. OTHERWISE, YOU WOULDN'T HAVE HOPPED ALONG TO CALIFORNIA WITH US.

MAYBE I JUST LIKED THE ADVENTURE.

OR MAYBE ARCHIE IS YOUR BEST FRIEND, JUGHEAD.

AND YOU WANT TO BE A PART OF SOMETHING BIG WITH HIM.

I DID. BUT THAT IDEA WENT OUT THE WINDOW, ALONG WITH OUR MAP, ON THE SECOND DAY OF THE TOUR.

NO, IT DIDN'T.

WE'RE ON THE CUSP OF SOMETHING REALLY BIG. YOU CAN BE A PART OF IT NOW, OR REGRET IT FOREVER. BUT THE ONLY PERSON STOPPING YOU IS YOU.

FUNNY TO HEAR YOU SAYING THIS, SEEING AS HOW YOU'VE BEEN TRASHING ARCHIE HARDER THAN ANYONE ELSE.

BEING CRITICAL ISN'T SINGULAR, YOU DOLT. I CRITICIZE *BECAUSE* I CARE. ARCHIE IS LUCKY TO HAVE ME AROUND.

AND HE WAS LUCKY TO HAVE *YOU*, TOO.

SO, JUST TO CONFIRM, *YOU*-- VERONICA LODGE-- WANT *ME*-- JUGHEAD JONES-- BACK IN THE BAND?

FOR THE GREATER GOOD.

I DUNNO.

WELL THAT'S TOO BAD. YOU'RE GONNA MISS ONE HECK OF AN ADVENTURE COMING UP.

WHADDYA MEAN?

I KNOW WHO OUR BIG SHOW IS WITH AT THE END OF THE TOUR. IT'S GONNA BE SOMETHING.

THEY JUST TOLD ME THAT YOU GUYS ARE IN THE **BATTLE OF THE BANDS** AT THE END OF THE TOUR.
Oh, YES!
PLAYING AGAINST
JOSIE AND THE PUSSYCATS
Oh, **NO**.
I'D WISH YOU LUCK, BUT I DON'T THINK **ANYTHING'S** GONNA HELP YOU WITH **THIS**.
TO BE CONTINUED...

THIS IS THE BEST WE'VE PLAYED. *EVER.*

WHICH, LET'S FACE IT-- ISN'T SAYING MUCH. WE'VE BARELY KEPT OURSELVES TOGETHER.

WE'VE HAD EVERY OPPORTUNITY HANDED TO US--PLAYING WITH *CHVRCHES, TEGAN AND SARA*--

DID I MENTION A WEIRD *MONKEES* DREAM?

NEVER MIND.

PLUS, FREAKIN' *BLONDIE* PRODUCED OUR FIRST RECORD!

BUT EACH STEP OF THE WAY, WE'VE STUMBLED-- MOSTLY BECAUSE OF CARROT TOP.

NOW WE HAVE A CHANCE TO MAKE IT RIGHT, THOUGH.

IT ALMOST MAKES ME LIKE THESE CLOWNS.

WELL, IT WAS NICE WHILE IT LASTED.

WOOOOOOO!! YEAH!!

THAT GOOD?

THAT *GREAT*, ARCH.

IT'S NOT OVER YET.

Oh, IT'S OVER. IT'S ALL OVER.

REGGIE IS RIGHT. WE KNEW THIS WOULDN'T LAST FOREVER.

SOMEONE ALSO KNEW THAT WE'D BE FACING OFF AGAINST ONE OF THE BIGGEST BANDS PLAYING.

WHAT ARE YOU SUGGESTING, DOLTHEAD?

HOOORAY!

PU-SSY-CATS! PU-SSY-CATS!

WE LOVE YOU, JOSIE!!

LET'S HAVE ANOTHER ROUND OF APPLAUSE FOR THE UNSTOPPABLE, AMAZING--

JOSIE AND THE PUSSY-CATS!!

PRETTY SURE OUR SHOT JUST MISFIRED.

GULP.

WELL, I WISH I COULD SAY IT'S BEEN REAL, BUT IT'S ACTUALLY BEEN--

REGGIE, MUTE.

WHAT NOW?

I GUESS WE GO BACK TO THE HOTEL AND GET SOME SLEEP. WE SHOULD ALSO TRY AND BOOK SOME SHOWS FOR THE WAY HOME.

CONGRATS, EVERYONE!

THANKS! YOU GUYS WERE AMAZING UP THERE.

NOT AMAZING ENOUGH, THOUGH.

HEY, VERONICA. CAN I TALK TO YOU FOR A SECOND?

WE WERE WONDERING WHAT YOU WERE DOING NOW?

I'M GONNA GO SOAK IN THE TUB FOR A YEAR OR FIVE.

NO, I MEANT, LIKE, MUSICALLY. YOU'RE REALLY GOOD.

AND WE'VE BEEN TALKING ABOUT ADDING A KEYBOARD PLAYER TO OUR BAND FOR A WHILE. SO...

I'M STILL IN **MY** BAND.

ARE YOU SURE?

LATER THAT NIGHT.

NOK NOK

GO AWAY, JUGHEAD! I ALREADY TOLD YOU, THEY CHARGE US FOR THE FOOD WE EAT FROM THE MINI-FRIDGES.

IT'S NOT "HIDDEN TREASURE."

Umm...

YOU'RE NOT JUGHEAD...

NOT LAST TIME I CHECKED, NO.

SADIE, RIGHT? I'M A BIG SPEEDY ORTIZ FAN.

YEAH. THAT'S ACTUALLY WHY I'M HERE. SORRY TO JUST SHOW UP, BUT THE BATTLE OF THE BANDS PUT US ALL UP IN THE SAME HOTEL AND I WANTED TO TALK TO YOU.

THIS IS WEIRD, SO I'M JUST GOING TO SAY IT.

YOU'RE A GREAT GUITARIST AND WE COULD USE A TOURING GUITARIST.

ANY CHANCE YOU'D WANT TO HIT THE ROAD WITH US FOR A BIT?

WOW. I...*WOW*. THAT'S AMAZING. BUT MY BAND IS TOURING HOME TOMORROW...

Oh, I'M SO SORRY. I HEARD YOU ALL BROKE UP TONIGHT...

Oh, GOOD. YOU'RE ALL HERE ALREADY.

YEAH. TIME TO HEAD HOME AND WRITE SOME NEW SONGS I GUESS.

YEAH... I'M NOT GOING.

WHAT?!

SHE JOINED JOSIE AND THE PUSSYCATS LAST NIGHT. SHE'S RECORDING THEIR ALBUM WITH THEM.

YOU'RE GOING TO WEAR THE EARS?

WE'RE STILL NEGOTIATING THAT. AND YES, I JOINED THE PUSSYCATS. IT JUST FELT LIKE THE RIGHT TIME TO MOVE ON.

ARE YOU MAD, ARCHIEKINS?

NO...

I MEAN, I WAS WHEN I HEARD LAST NIGHT. BUT I UNDER-STAND.

AND I'M NOT GOING EITHER.

SPEEDY ORTIZ ASKED ME TO BE THEIR TOURING GUITARIST.

FINE. IT'S JUST THE THREE OF US THEN. THAT'S OKAY. WE--

ACTUALLY, I BOUGHT A PLANE TICKET LAST NIGHT. I CALLED UP DILTON, ETHEL AND TONI BACK IN RIVERDALE, AND I'M RESTARTING REGGIE AND THE REGGIES. MY GENIUS CAN'T WAIT.

JUST YOU AND ME, BETTS.

ACTUALLY...

I WAS GOING TO HANG AROUND L.A. FOR A BIT.

I SAW AN AD FOR OPEN MIC NIGHT AT A BAR IN LOS FELIZ.

I HAVE A WHOLE BUNCH OF SONGS AND I JUST WANT TO PLAY THEM IN A PLACE WHERE NOBODY KNOWS ME.

I'M SORRY.

JUST ME THEN, I GUESS.

Oh, MAN. IS THAT OKAY?

YEAH. THERE'S A TON OF BURGER SPOTS THAT NONE OF YOU'D WANT TO GO TO THAT I WANTED TO HIT ON THE WAY HOME ANYWAY.

SO...WHAT DOES THIS MEAN?

TWO DAYS LATER.

♪ AND THAT'S ALL YOU'LL EVER KNOOOOW! ♪

THANKS SO MUCH FOR...NOT SNORING TOO LOUD. I'M BETTY COOPER AND I'LL BE PLAYING HERE EVERY NIGHT. TELL YOUR FRIENDS.

THAT WAS GREAT.

HEY, THANKS. I TAKE IT YOU WEREN'T THE GUY WHO THREW UP?

NO. YOU KNOW I HATE TO THROW UP IN FRONT OF YOU.

ARCHIE?! I THOUGHT YOU WERE ALREADY ON THE ROAD!

NO, I TOLD SADIE I HAD TO SEE SOMETHING HERE BEFORE I COULD GO.

ARCHIEKINS IS RIGHT. YOU WERE GREAT.

RONNIE?!

DON'T ACT SO SURPRISED. WE'RE REHEARSING JUST UP THE STREET.

BESIDES, I WASN'T GOING TO MISS YOUR BIG SOLO SHOW.

EH, IT WASN'T MUCH OF A SOLO SHOW.

THAT'S TRUE. BUT IT WASN'T ANY WORSE THAN MOST OF *OUR* SHOWS.

REGGIE, YOU STAYED TOO!

WHAT? NO. MY FLIGHT WAS CANCELLED BECAUSE OF BAD WEATHER.

I STAYED. I WANTED TO SEE YOU PLAY.

AWW, THANKS, JUGGIE!

IT'S NO BIG DEAL. I HAVE THE VAN. I CAN LEAVE WHENEVER. JUST A SHORT 3,000 MILE DRIVE HOME.

WELL, WELL, WELL. WOULDJA LOOK AT US. FIVE EX-MEMBERS OF THE ARCHIES ON STAGE AGAIN. HOW LONG HAS IT BEEN?

FORTY-ONE HOURS.

LOOK AT ALL THIS GEAR, ALL SET UP. IT'S A SHAME NOT TO USE IT. YOU WANT TO PLAY SOMETHING WHILE WE'RE ALL UP HERE?

THE BAR'S CLOSED, ARCHIE. THERE'S NO ONE LEFT TO PLAY FOR.

NO...

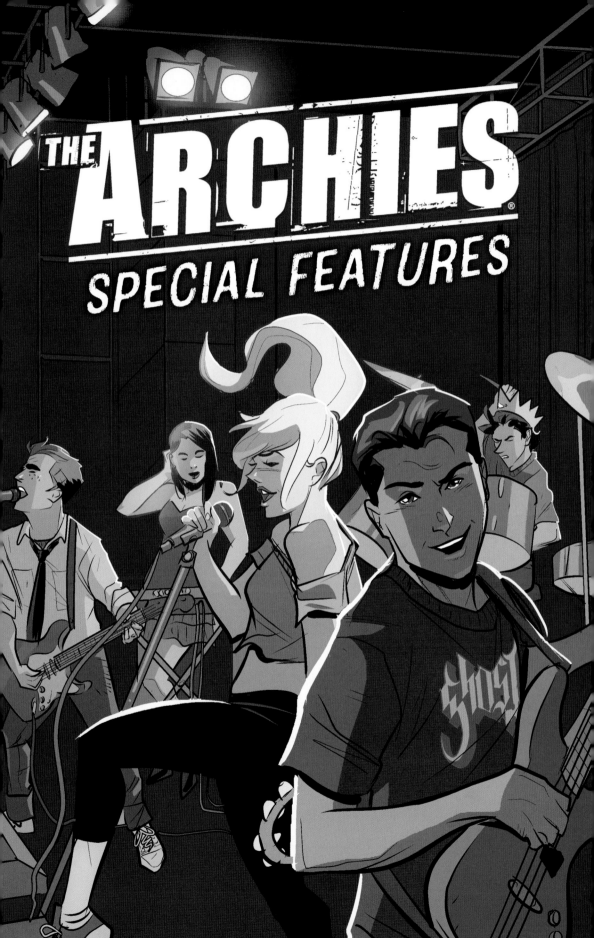

THE ARCHIES

COVER GALLERY

ISSUE FOUR

GREG SMALLWOOD

MIKE AND LAURA ALLRED

JOE EISMA

ISSUE FIVE

GREG SMALLWOOD

JOE EISMA

THOMAS PITILLI

ISSUE SIX

GREG SMALLWOOD

DAN PARENT

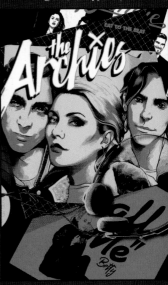

MATTHEW TAYLOR

ISSUE SEVEN

GREG SMALLWOOD

CLIFF CHIANG

FIONA STAPLES

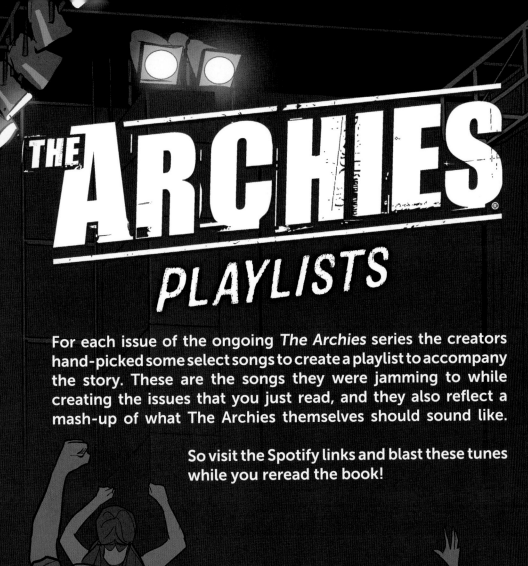

THE ARCHIES

PLAYLISTS

For each issue of the ongoing *The Archies* series the creators hand-picked some select songs to create a playlist to accompany the story. These are the songs they were jamming to while creating the issues that you just read, and they also reflect a mash-up of what The Archies themselves should sound like.

So visit the Spotify links and blast these tunes while you reread the book!

THE ARCHIES ISSUE #4 PLAYLIST

"BLUE PERIOD" - THE SMITHEREENS

"JUST WHAT I NEEDED" - THE CARS

"CRUEL TO BE KIND" - NICK LOWE

"VERONICA" - ELVIS COSTELLO

"SURRENDER" - CHEAP TRICK

"WHAT DO I GET?" - BUZZCOCKS

"I WANNA BE FREE" - THE MONKEES

"PUT YOUR MONEY ON ME" - THE STRUTS

"CHEAPSKATE" - SUPERGRASS

"STREET FIGHTING MAN" - THE ROLLING STONES

"OH MY HEART" - NIGHT RIOTS

"SHE'S SO HOT" - THE MADCAPS

LISTEN ON OUR SPOTIFY PLAYLIST AT:
http://bit.ly/TheArchies4  Spotify®

THE ARCHIES ISSUE #5 PLAYLIST

"HERE SHE COMES NOW" - VELVET UNDERGROUND

"SPEAK FOR ME" - CAT POWER

"HERE COMES THE NEW BRUNETTE" - BILLY BRAGG

"GET UP OFFA THAT THING" - JAMES BROWN

"THE SKY LIT UP" - PJ HARVEY

"DIRTY WORK" - STEELY DAN

"BROKEN BONES" - CHVRCHES

"STATE OF MIND" - SATCHMODE

"FOOD FOR THE BEAST" - NINA PERSSON

"HERE SHE COMES" - THE WHY OH WHYS

"LIVING & DYING FOR" - MINT

"STOP DESIRE" - TEGAN & SARA

LISTEN ON OUR SPOTIFY PLAYLIST AT:
http://bit.ly/TheArchies5

THE ARCHIES ISSUE #6 PLAYLIST

"YOUNG LOVER" - ST. VINCENT
"NO BELOW" - SPEEDY ORTIZ
"SUNDAY GIRL" - BLONDIE
"SHE'S NOT ME" - JENNY LEWIS
"NO ACTION" - ELVIS COSTELLO
AND THE ATTRACTIONS
"HEARTBEAT" - BAT FANGS
"BAD FUN" - COURTSHIP
"SHE TAUGHT ME HOW TO FLY"
- NOEL GALLAGHER'S HIGH FLYING BIRDS
"COME THROUGH" - THE REGRETTES
"A VERY SPECIAL SONG FOR A VERY
SPECIAL YOUNG LADY PT 2." - THE ERGS
"VALERIE LOVES ME" - MATERIAL ISSUE
"HUGO" - TOO MUCH JOY
"AN HONEST ROMANCE" - PAWS
"20, 21" - SCREAM HELLO

LISTEN ON OUR SPOTIFY PLAYLIST AT:
http://bit.ly/TheArchies6

THE ARCHIES ISSUE #7 PLAYLIST

"SESAME" - TOUCHE AMORE

"DOWN FOR MY PEOPLE LIKE JOE CARROLL"

- BRIDGE AND TUNNEL

"TURN IT OFF" - CULTURE ABUSE

"BEGINNING IN AN ENDING" - AGAINST ME!

"UNPLUGGED" - VOKES

"YOU DON'T GET IT'" - HARLEA

"THE EDGE OF FOREVER" - WORK DRUGS

"AFTER HOURS" - THE VELVET UNDERGROUND

"BASKETBALL" - SPEEDY ORTIZ

"I KNOW IT'S OVER" - THE SMITHS

"LET IT BLEED" - THE ROLLING STONES

LISTEN ON OUR SPOTIFY PLAYLIST AT:
http://bit.ly/TheArchies7  Spotify®

THE ARCHIES

EASTER EGGS

The Archies not only featured a variety of real-world band cameos as well as playlists curated by writers Alex Segura and Matthew Rosenberg, it also featured a number of Easter Eggs that many music aficionados will appreciate.

Writer Alex Segura said, "One of the best parts about working on THE ARCHIES comic book series was having not only amazing, real-life musical guest stars like CHVRCHES, Speedy Ortiz and Tegan and Sara, but weaving a bunch of hat tips and Easter Eggs to all the bands we (artist Joe Eisma and co-writer Matthew Rosenberg) love—from Oasis to Waxahatchee, you'll find nods to every era of music. It's a love letter to the sounds that inspired us while we worked on the book."

DID YOU SPOT ALL THE REAL LIFE BANDS ON ARCHIE'S GUITAR CASE FROM THE COVER OF THE ARCHIES #5?

The Ramones, KISS, Radiohead, Chvrches, The Pixies, The Monkees, Agent Orange, Rancid

THERE ARE EVEN MORE MUSICAL HAT TIPS THROUGHOUT THE INTERIORS OF ISSUES 4 AND 5, FROM THE CHARACTERS' SHIRTS TO A CONCERT POSTER:

TONITE!
The ARCHIES
(ON TOUR FROM RIVERDALE!)
PIs
(CHICAGO'S OWN)
WILCO
(FROM HERE!)
WESLEY WILLIS
(FROM HERE!)
PLUS SPECIAL GUESTS:
The MONKEES
(FROM ARCHIE'S WEIRD DREAM!)
$5. 8PM.
ALL AGES.

Fenix TX, CHVRCHES, PIs, Wilco, Wesley Willis, Missing Persons

Night Moves, The Struts, The Why Oh Whys, Black Flag

ARCHIE AND THE GANG HAVE EVEN MORE BAND SHIRTS IN ISSUES 6 AND 7:

Duran Duran, Mac Sabbath, Ghost

Waxahatchee, Gorillaz, The Mountain Goats